MW00699005

Purgatory

A Mystery of Love

by
Fr. Donncha Ó hAodha

*All booklets are published thanks to the
generous support of the members of the
Catholic Truth Society*

Contents

ISBN 978 1 78469 046 5

The Christian's Calling

See what love the Father has given us, that we should be called children of God; and so we are...Beloved we are God's children now; it does not yet appear what we shall be, but we know that when he appears we shall be like him, for we shall see him as he is. And every one who thus hopes in him purifies himself as he is pure (1 Jn 3:1-3).

All who die in God's grace and friendship, but still imperfectly purified, are indeed assured of their eternal salvation; but after death they undergo purification, so as to achieve the holiness necessary to enter the joy of heaven (Catechism of the Catholic Church 1030).

Baptism: A Call to Grace

The greatness and dignity of the Christian vocation is beyond what we can grasp fully because God's love for us in Christ is infinite. The identity of the baptised as a "new creation" (*2 Co* 5:17), as "sharers in the divine nature" (*2 P* 1:4) totally surpasses anything human beings could imagine or hope for. It is not surprising that St Paul prays for the Ephesians that the eyes of their hearts may be enlightened so that they may know what is the hope to which God has called them (cf. *Ep* 1:18). Indeed the entire life of the Catholic might be seen as the attempt to deepen in the awareness of God's love and to respond accordingly.

In Baptism, by the infusion of sanctifying grace we become children of God the Father, in Christ by the Holy Spirit. This is a genuine transformation which makes us sons or daughters in the Son (cf. *Rm* 8:14-17). St John teaches the reality of this mystery in his first letter: "See what love the Father has given us, that we should be called children of God; and so we are" (3:1). St John stresses that we are not just "called children of God" but that "we are" truly such. St Athanasius expressed this "divinisation" of man with the phrase: "The Son of God became man so that we might become God".[1]

This identification with Christ is real and is destined to grow throughout our lives. Our participation in the mystery of Christ is the basis for the universal call to holiness (cf. *Rm* 6:5-11). As the Second Vatican Council teaches: "Justified in the Lord Jesus, because in the baptism of faith they truly become sons of God and sharers in the divine nature [the followers of Christ] are really made holy. Then too, by God's gift, they must hold on to and complete in their lives this holiness they have received...Thus it is evident to everyone, that all the faithful of Christ of whatever rank or status, are called to the fullness of the Christian life and to the perfection of charity".[2] God's love for us is unconditional and invites us in return to trust and love him unconditionally.

The Battle for Holiness

To grow in holiness, to enable Christ to be formed in us (cf. *Ga* 4:19), we must freely collaborate with the work of grace by our ongoing response to the love of God which constantly invites us to communion with the Trinity. The call addressed to each and every member of the faithful is wonderful and demanding: "You are to be perfect as your heavenly Father is perfect" (*Mt* 5:48). This requires constant vigilance and the effort to improve. As St John explains, "everyone who thus hopes in him purifies himself as he is pure" (*1 Jn* 3:3).

The battle for holiness does not depend exclusively on human effort, nor is it a lonesome business. Along the journey of the Christian life we are never lacking divine help, especially through the sacraments. We are strengthened by Confirmation and constantly purified and renewed, especially by the sacraments of Penance and the Eucharist.

To enter into communion with the all-holy God in everlasting life we too need to be holy. As St John Paul II explained, "every trace of attachment to evil must be eliminated, every imperfection of the soul corrected. Purification must be complete, and indeed this is precisely what is meant by the Church's teaching on *Purgatory*".[3] For those faithful who die in friendship with God but not yet entirely purified, the mercy of God provides a last cleansing of love which enables them to embrace the fullness of Love. This is Purgatory.

Far from being an isolated or insignificant dogma, Purgatory speaks of the fundamental reality of God's relationship with the baptised, having raised them to the immense dignity of becoming his children in Christ. Purgatory highlights the vocation of all to achieve their full human and spiritual potential through the progressive identification with Christ which is holiness. Purgatory evokes what Benedict XVI indicated as "one of the fundamental themes of humanity's religious history: the question of the purity of the human being before God".[4] It also implies the importance of justice, for God, for man, and for the entire creation.

The doctrine of Purgatory also points to the consoling reality of the Church as the Communion of Saints. "It is the reality of a family bound together by deep bonds of spiritual solidarity that unites the faithful departed to those who are pilgrims in the world. It is a mysterious but real bond, nourished by prayer and participation in the Sacrament of the Eucharist."[5] The three dimensions of the Church, in heaven, on earth, and undergoing purification after death, are shown to be truly united in light of the mystery of Purgatory.

The Existence of Purgatory

Sacred Scripture

In his catechesis on Purgatory of 4th August 1999, St John Paul II pointed out that Scripture "contains certain elements that help to understand the meaning of this doctrine, even if it is not formally described".[6] While having a solid biblical basis, because the Church deepened in her understanding of this truth over time, it is not surprising that a developed doctrine is not to be found in sacred Scripture.

The scriptural evidence for Purgatory can be shown in two ways. Firstly, this dogma is a necessary consequence of fundamental biblical teachings about the nature of God and of man. Secondly, Purgatory can be asserted with reference to specific texts.

Fundamental biblical foundations for Purgatory:
divine holiness and justice

To see Purgatory within the broad perspective of the relationship between God and man helps to situate this truth within the entirety of the Faith. Specifically, two great biblical themes might be considered: divine holiness, which requires absolute purity in the person who would enter God's company; and divine justice, which implies human responsibility for sin and the consequent personal contribution towards reconciliation through making-up, expiation or reparation.

Throughout Scripture the all-holy God commands his people to be holy because he is holy,[7] and as he is holy.[8] The fundamental principle whereby only those fully purified may approach the All-pure is frequently stated, such as in Psalm 15:1-2: "O Lord, who shall sojourn in your tent? Who shall dwell on thy holy hill? He who walks blamelessly, and does what is right, and speaks truth from his heart".[9] The detailed ceremonial of Old Testament worship of God aimed at impeding any unclean person or object from coming into the presence of God, even if it were merely legal impurities.[10]

The New Testament ratifies this demand for total purity, not only by announcing God's will for man's holiness,[11] but also by confirming it as a prerequisite for participating in eternal life, as Christ himself teaches: "Blessed are the pure in heart for they shall see God" (*Mt* 5:8).

The demand of total holiness

The first printed homily of Blessed John Henry Newman, delivered when he was twenty-five years old, was entitled 'The Holiness necessary for future Blessedness'. Here he meditated on "the holiness without which no one will see the Lord" (*Heb* 12:14).[12] Newman asks why it is that God demands total holiness given that man is obviously weak and prone to sin. Might this not be too demanding on God's part?

"I answer as follows", says Newman, "that, even supposing a man of unholy life were suffered to enter heaven, *he would not be happy there*; so that it would be no mercy to permit him to enter."

In fact, the call to holiness is not at all an unreasonable demand, but a fruit of God's love. We are called to reach maturity in the identity we received at baptism as beloved children of the Father.[13] For this reason, as Newman points out, "heaven is *not* heaven, is not a place of happiness *except* to the holy."

The process of Christian holiness which involves progressive purification is not always completed in this life. In his love, the Lord offers a final cleansing. "Those who die in God's grace and friendship imperfectly purified…undergo a purification after death, so as to achieve the holiness necessary to enter the joy of God."[14]

Divine justice

A second great biblical foundation for Purgatory is divine justice, whereby the sinner makes up for his or her sin. This "reparation" which respects the demands of justice and also of human dignity, brings about the "atonement" which makes the sinner to be "at-one" with God again.

A case in point is that of King David (cf. *2 S* 11-12). Having taken Bethsheba, wife of Uriah the Hittite, unlawfully to himself, David subsequently brings about the death of her husband. The prophet Nathan is sent by the Lord to face David with his crime.[15] In reply to the king's confession of guilt, the prophet informs David that the Lord has forgiven his sin, but that he must expiate that evil:

"And Nathan said to David, 'The Lord also has put away your sin; you shall not die. Nevertheless, because by this deed you have utterly scorned the Lord, the child that is born to you shall die'" (*2 S* 12:13-14).

One might also cite Numbers 12:14 ff., which tells of the expiation of Miriam, Moses' sister, for her sin, or Numbers 20:12, where it is clear that the pardon of Moses' sin does not exempt him from the penance of not leading the people into the Promised Land.

The same teaching abounds in the New Testament. Zacchaeus is truly forgiven and he also makes amends: "Behold, Lord, the half of my goods I give to the poor; and if I have defrauded any one of anything, I restore it fourfold" (*Lk* 19:8). The Risen Lord asks Peter three times if he loves him.[16] In this way, Peter is given the opportunity to freely atone for his triple denial of the Lord.[17]

As the *Catechism of the Catholic Church* explains, every sin has *"a double consequence.* Grave sin deprives us of communion with God", while less serious or venial sins weaken that communion. Also, "every sin, even venial, entails an unhealthy attachment to creatures, which must be purified either here on earth or after death in the state called Purgatory. This punishment frees one from what is called the 'temporal punishment' of sin".[18]

It is important to emphasise that making up for sin is not a matter of placating a vengeful God, but rather of respecting justice, and freely assuming, in accordance with our dignity as children of God, the consequences of our sins. As the *Catechism* points out, the unhealthy attachment to creatures and temporal punishment which result from sin, "must not be conceived of as a kind of vengeance inflicted by God from without, but as following from the very nature of sin".[19]

Specific biblical texts

There are two key scriptural texts for Purgatory, one in the Old Testament and the other in the New.

2 Maccabees

2 Maccabees 12:39-45 recounts the actions of Judas Maccabeus and his troops after their victory over Gorgias, governor of Idumea. When they went to collect the bodies of their fallen, "under the tunic of every one of

the dead they found sacred tokens of the idols of Jamnia
which the law forbids the Jews to wear" (v. 40). Realising
that these comrades had died in this sin, the survivors
"turned to prayer, beseeching that the sin which had
been committed might be wholly blotted out" (v. 42).
Moreover, Judas "took up a collection, man by man, to
the amount of two thousand drachmas of silver, and sent
it to Jerusalem to provide for a sin offering" (v. 43).

This Old Testament passage is significant because it
shows the belief that these men had died guilty of a sin
which did not preclude them from heaven, and that the
living could intercede for the benefit of the dead, also
by offering a sacrifice of expiation on their behalf. This
sacred text explicitly ratifies Judas's action in having a
sacrifice offered for the dead. "In doing this he acted
very well and honourably (v. 43) ... He made atonement
for the dead that they might be delivered from their
sin" (v. 45).

The importance of this text for the Church's faith in
Purgatory is heightened by the reference made to it by
Church Fathers[20] and the Magisterium.[21]

1 Corinthians

1 Corinthians 3:12-15 is also fundamental to Catholic
reflection on Purgatory. Indeed, its interpretations down
through the centuries constitute to a great degree a history
of theological reflection on purification after death.

In this text St Paul addresses himself to the community he had founded at Corinth. The Apostle compares the teachers of the faith at Corinth to builders or architects who, by their preaching, construct on the only foundation, laid by St Paul himself, "which is Christ Jesus" (v. 11).

Now if any one builds on the foundation with gold, silver, precious stones, wood, hay, stubble - each man's work will become manifest; for the Day will disclose it, because it will be revealed with fire, and the fire will test what sort of work each has done. If the work which any man has built on the foundation survives, he will receive a reward. If any man's work is burned up, he will suffer loss though he himself will be saved, but only as through fire (vv. 12-15).

Those who build on the foundation of Christ with "gold, silver, precious stones" are those who teach solid doctrine for the glory of God and the benefit of their listeners, while those who use "wood, hay, stubble" teach vain but not heretical doctrine. Their teaching is poor but does not destroy its ultimate foundation.

All these teachers will be judged on the "day" of reckoning (v. 12) and receive their just recompense. Because they have not abandoned the ultimate foundation-stone which is Christ, their souls are safe, but those whose work was deficient "will be saved, but only as through fire" (v. 15).

The Church Fathers

Much of the reflection by the Church Fathers on Purgatory is found in their consideration of this Pauline teaching. While not regarded as a direct and explicit reference, the text is seen as an indirect affirmation of the doctrine.

Thus Clement of Alexandria (d. before 215) and Origen (d. 253/4) focused on the judgement of souls by fire suggested by this text. The Cappadochian Fathers, Sts Basil (d. 379), Gregory of Nazianzen (d. c. 390) and Gregory of Nyssa (d. 394) also reflected on purification in the next life in light of 1 Corinthians 3:12-15.[22]

Throughout the history of the Church several other biblical texts have also been cited in relation to Purgatory, but here we will refer only to two more.

In Matthew 12:32, the Lord affirms that "whoever speaks against the Holy Spirit will not be forgiven, either in this age or in the age to come". Some Church Fathers have suggested a basis for Purgatory here, in so far as the text seems to suggest that some sins can be removed after death.[23]

The admonition in Luke 12:58-59, and its parallel text in Matthew 5:25-26, has also been invoked. Here the Lord recommends making peace with one's accuser along the way, to avoid being dragged to the judge, and thrown into prison from which - "I tell you, you will never get out till you have paid the last very last copper" (*Lk* 12:59).

In his great counter-Reformation defence of Purgatory,[24] St Robert Bellarmine takes up the patristic[25] heritage which sees these words of the Gospel as an allusion to the soul who dies with unpardoned venial sins or a debt of temporal punishment due to sin.[26] In this sense the "prison" spoken of (v. 58) would be identified with Purgatory.

Sacred Tradition

The gradual development of the Church's understanding of Purgatory has been complex, so that it is impossible to give a detailed account of it here. The Church deepened in her faith in Purgatory in an organic way. The reflection of the Fathers was primarily based on their study of Scripture, while from the very beginning the praxis of prayer for the dead testified both to the doctrine of Scripture and nurtured the teaching of theologians.

Here we will look briefly at sacred Tradition as expressed in two fundamental ways; in the writings of the Fathers of the Church, and in the sacred Liturgy.

Patristic thought

The visions of St Perpetua recorded in the account of her martyrdom along with St Felicity, constitute one of the earliest testimonies of the Latin tradition regarding Purgatory. These two women suffered martyrdom on 7th March 203, under the emperor Septimus Severus, and the text describing their passion dates from the start of the third century.[27]

Imprisoned for her faith, before being thrown to wild beasts, St Perpetua has two visions of her younger brother Dinocrates who had died from an illness. In the first vision St Perpetua sees her brother coming out from a dark place, pale-faced and covered with dirt, and suffering from an immense thirst because of the stifling heat. He is unable however to reach the fountain of water above him. The saint, touched by her deceased brother's state, prays intensely for him to the Lord and in a later vision Perpetua sees Dinocrates clean, well-dressed and relieved, playing as a child and radiant with joy. Her conclusion is: "Then I understood that he had been moved from the place of suffering". Her prayers and sacrifices had benefited her deceased brother in his purification.

Much of the Fathers' teaching emphasises the need to pray for the dead for the alleviation of their sufferings and to speed their entry to heaven. For example in his work *De Monogamia*, Tertullian (d. after 220) describes how the faithful widow "prays for the soul of her husband…and offers [the Mass] on the anniversary days of his death".[28]

In a letter he wrote to Pammachius to console him on the death of his wife Paulina, St Jerome (d. 419/420) stresses how giving alms to the needy can aid those who have died. "Other husbands strew violets, roses…on the graves of their wives, and soothe with these offices the sorrow of their hearts; our Pammachius bedews the hallowed dust and venerable remains of Paulina with balsams of alms. With these pigments and sweet odours does he refresh her slumbering ashes, knowing that it is written, that as water quenches fire, so do alms extinguish sin".[29]

As with so many other aspects of Catholic doctrine, the contribution of St Augustine (d. 430) was very significant. He stressed that immediately after death the soul's eternal destiny is fixed: those fully purified enter heaven, those condemned enter hell, and those who need it undergo a period of purification before entering glory.

The Eastern Church

While in the West, the idea of Purgatory developed in its initial stages with almost no connection with ancient philosophy, this was not the case in the East. Specifically, Clement of Alexandria's (d. before 215) thought was worked out in debate with Gnosticism, and within the context of Greek philosophical thought.

Clement sees Christian existence as a whole in terms of the Greek idea of *paideia* or "education". Man is "divinised", becomes a sharer in the divine life, at baptism. The process of maturing in holiness continues throughout life and reaches into eternity. With reference to 1 Corinthians 3:12-15, Clement speaks of a fire after death which purifies and "educates" the individual for heavenly glory. Those undergoing this process of purification can be helped by the prayers of other members of the Church.

Referring to Clement's thought on Purgatory, Joseph Ratzinger makes the point that in the East, in a quite different context, "we meet again the two basic elements of the idea of purgatory which we saw emerge by gradual development in the West".[30] These two aspects are the affirmation of the existence of Purgatory, and the value of "suffrages" or helps which can be offered by the living faithful for the dead.

The Liturgy

The *Catechism of the Catholic Church* teaches that "liturgy is a constitutive element of the holy and living Tradition."[31] In other words the Liturgy is a true expression of the Church's faith. Hence the ancient Christian adage: *lex orandi, lex credendi*: "the law of prayer is the law of faith".

This is very clear in regard to Purgatory since from the very beginning and without interruption the Church has always prayed for the dead, especially during the Eucharistic sacrifice. Prayer for the repose of the faithful departed is found in all liturgical traditions, such as those of Jerusalem, Rome, Alexandria, Ethiopia, Milan, and in the liturgies of St Basil, St John Chrysostom, St Gregory the Great, St Cyril and the Mozarabic liturgy of Spain.

In the Eastern tradition, St Cyril of Jerusalem (d. 386) witnesses to prayer for the dead at Mass: "We commemorate...all who have already fallen asleep from among us, believing that it will be a very great assistance to the souls for which the supplication is put up, while the holy and most awful sacrifice lies open to view".[32]

From the Western Church, St Augustine gives a personal and moving testimony to the same faith when he recalls the words of his dying mother St Monica: "Lay this body anywhere; let not the care of it anyway disturb you; this only I ask of you, that you would remember me at the altar of God wherever you be". St Augustine recalls the funeral Mass of his mother as he addresses the Lord in his *Confessions*: "Neither in those prayers which we poured forth unto Thee when the sacrifice of our ransom was offered for her...not even in those prayers did I weep".[33]

Prayers for the departed

Statements of the Magisterium on the efficacy of prayer for the dead, and especially of the Mass as the principal suffrage or aid for the holy souls,[34] give expression to the faith of the Church as practised in the Liturgy from the very beginning, always and everywhere.

Christian archaeology also bears out the belief that the deceased can benefit from the support of others' prayers. Countless ancient funeral inscriptions entrust the dead to the mercy of God, or appeal to the living to pray for the person interred in a given tomb. Some such engraved prayers address the dead person directly.

There are numerous examples, of which the following might be mentioned: "May you live in the Lord Jesus!" (*Vivas in Domine Iesu!*), "May you live in God and intercede [for us]!" (*Vivas in Deo et roga!*), or "May you [plural] be at peace!" (*In pace estote!*).[35]

The Christian tradition of burying the dead near the graves of martyrs and saints - one thinks of the concentration of burials around that of St Peter on the Vatican hill - also shows faith in the intercession of the saints for the souls of the faithful departed.

Christian cemeteries thus reflect the awareness of the communion that exists between the heavenly Church, the earthly or pilgrim Church, and the Church of Purgatory, those "who rest in the sleep of peace"[36] in the certainty of their entry to glory.

The Nature of Purgatory

The Teaching of the Church

The Church has defined two fundamental truths about Purgatory, namely its existence, and the capacity of the living to aid the dead, especially by offering the Mass.

In the face of the Lutheran denial of Purgatory, the Council of Trent reaffirmed this teaching in several places. Specifically in the great doctrinal decree 'On Justification', Trent asserted the need to expiate the debt of temporal punishment due to sin, either in this life or in Purgatory.[37] Towards its conclusion, this Council also issued a brief 'Decree on Purgatory'. While more disciplinary than dogmatic in character, in its exhortation to all the bishops of the Church, the decree recalls the basic teaching:

> Since the Catholic Church, instructed by the Holy Spirit, in conformity with the sacred writings and ancient traditions of the Fathers in sacred councils and very recently in this ecumenical Synod, has taught that there is a purgatory, and that the souls detained

there are assisted by the suffrages of the faithful, and especially by the acceptable sacrifice of the altar, the holy Synod commands the bishops that they insist that the sound doctrine of purgatory, which has been transmitted by the holy Fathers and the holy Councils, be believed by the faithful of Christ, be maintained, taught and everywhere preached.[38]

The Church has been sober in what she has defined about Purgatory. Further aspects of the doctrine can be deduced from its fundamental nucleus. There is ample space for theological reflection on this mystery of faith in light of Church teaching. In dealing with "the last things", there is also a danger of imagining or speculating on "things that tend to a certain curiosity or superstition",[39] a tendency explicitly discouraged by the Council of Trent.

Nonetheless it makes sense to reflect on Purgatory, as on every other aspect of Revelation, and all the more so since this dogma touches on such a fundamental question as eternal life. Indeed as Vatican II points out, "it is in the face of death that the riddle of human existence becomes most acute".[40]

A healthy and fruitful reflection on Purgatory is possible when carried out in the light of Scripture and Tradition and with the mind of the Church, Further as St John Paul pointed out, to deepen in the Catholic faith, "we are greatly helped not only by theological investigation but also by that great heritage which is *"the 'lived theology' of the saints."*[41]

The State of the Holy Souls

The *Catechism of the Catholic Church* teaches that "each man receives his eternal retribution in his immortal soul at the very moment of his death, in a particular judgement that refers his life to Christ: either entrance to the blessedness of heaven - through a purification or immediately, or immediate and everlasting damnation."[42]

This statement of Catholic faith is followed by the fundamental criterion for judgement as formulated by St John of the Cross: "At the evening of life, we shall be judged on our love."[43]

Purgatory is then a purification of love. Those who undergo this final cleansing after death have indeed died in the love of God, but that love is not yet perfect. More specifically the holiness of these souls may be tarnished by unforgiven venial sins, evil inclinations or temporal punishment due to sin.

In this context of the "matter" of the souls' purification the main reason why Luther and other Protestant leaders denied the doctrine of Purgatory may be understood.

Luther's teaching, sometimes termed "extrinsic justification", is that the human person is not actually touched or transformed by the grace of Baptism, but is just declared by God to be saved in virtue of Christ's merits. In this view, the human person is not in fact changed at all interiorly by divine grace and can be saved only by an act of faith in Christ as their Saviour. Because the Christian has no real participation in the life of grace, he or she does not grow progressively in holiness. Rather it is a question of making a faith-filled act of trust in God or not making it, hence choosing heaven or hell. Just as there is no interior growth in holiness in this life, there is no reason for personal purification in the next.

Catholic teaching on Purgatory is fundamentally incompatible with this original Lutheran conception of a salvation purely "from the outside", with no intrinsic renewal by the Holy Spirit. Justification or salvation seen as a purely external declaration that one is saved by Christ, leaves no space for personal purification here or hereafter.

Nonetheless Luther did not deny Purgatory immediately. Initially he continued to accept it. Under the insistence of Zwingli however he came to teach in 1519 that it is not to be found in Scripture. This affirmation led him, among other things, to claim that 2 Maccabees, with its classic text on this topic, did not belong to the canon of Sacred Scripture. In 1524 he taught that the Mass should not be offered for the dead. In 1530 he wrote a *Refutation of Purgatory* on the occasion of the Diet of Augsburg, while he again denied the existence of Purgatory, in quite strident tones, in the 1537 *Smalcald Articles*.

The teaching of the Council of Trent has already been alluded to. The fundamental response to Lutheran doctrine is to be found in its *Decree on Justification*. In reaffirming the Church's belief that the faithful are truly renewed by baptismal grace, Trent was asserting the doctrinal foundation for Purgatory. If the work of sanctification is not completed in this life the process can be completed in the next by the mercy of God.

Purifying Suffering

During our earthly lives we can be purified by means of the sacraments, prayer and good works because God lovingly associates his children with his work of grace, and allows them to merit an increase in holiness and make "satisfaction" for their sins.[44]

However "death puts an end to human life as the time open to either accepting or rejecting the divine grace manifested in Christ".[45] Thus the holy souls in Purgatory can no longer actively "satisfy" for their sins. They can no longer merit, and so do not purify themselves; rather they are purified.

This purifying suffering of love is called "satispassion". This term comes from the Latin words *satis* meaning "enough" and *passio* which means "suffering". The holy souls do not "make satisfaction" (*satis-facere*) for their sins and faults. Instead they expiate their sins by undergoing purifying suffering which re-establishes holiness and justice. The souls "suffer" or undergo their cleansing. While they cannot actively make atonement, they joyfully embrace their final preparation for heaven, with faith, hope and love.

Given the passive aspect of the state of the holy souls, Purgatory has sometimes been referred to as a "crucible of love". It is not surprising that in Christian reflection scriptural images of the refining of metals have been applied to the purification of souls by God. For example, Malachi 3:2-3 says that the Lord "is like a refiner's fire and like fuller's soap; he will sit as a refiner and purifier of silver, and he will purify the sons of Levi and refine them like gold and silver, till they present right offerings to the Lord."

The state of the souls in Purgatory is decidedly intermediate. They are no longer in the earthly state of free decision and testing; they are no longer *in via* (on the way). Nor are they at home, *in patria*, in the house of the Father, although they know they will certainly reach there.

St Robert Bellarmine expresses their situation metaphorically. The soul in Purgatory is like a person who reaches a city in the dead of night. It can rightly be said that he has finished his journey and arrived, yet the doors remain closed until sunrise.[46]

Change is the Work of God

One of the most striking and beautiful meditations on the holy souls is the so-called *Treatise on Purgatory* by St Catherine of Genoa.[47] Catherine (1447-1510) was born to a noble family and married to an aristocrat Giuliano Adorno. On the occasion of her Lenten confession in 1473 she experienced a special grace which led her to greatly deepen her love of God. Her husband, who had not always been exemplary, also had a profound conversion and accompanied his wife for the rest of their days in caring for the poor and sick at the vast Pammatone Hospital in Genoa. Catherine was canonised by Pope Clement XII in 1737.

In his catechesis on this saint, Benedict XVI said:

It is important to note that Catherine, in her mystical experience, never received specific revelations on purgatory or on the souls being purified there. Yet, in the writings inspired by our Saint, purgatory is a central element and the description of it has characteristics that were original in her time.[48]

In her *Treatise*, Catherine repeatedly insists that no words or metaphors could adequately convey this mystery. In describing the state of the souls undergoing purgation, she affirms:

"The last stage of love is that which comes about and does its work without man's doing...If we are to become perfect, the change must be brought about in us and without us; that is, the change is to be the work not of man but of God."[49]

The Suffering of Purgatory

While the Church has declared nothing about the specific nature of the pains of Purgatory, it is clear that the greatest suffering is the delay of the beatific vision, in other words the postponement of seeing God face-to-face, which is heaven. The human being, made for eternal life with God suffers immensely on being delayed in this union with the ultimate object of all his or her desiring.

Moreover the holy souls are aware of the immense good of which they are temporarily deprived and conscious of their personal responsibility for this delay. They embrace this temporary and cleansing pain lovingly and in complete conformity with the will of God. The great twentieth century apologist Frank Sheed explains purgatorial sufferings with reference to sin:

> The acceptance of suffering is a reversal of the process of sin. For sin is the thrust of one's own will against God's. The total acceptance of God's will at whatever cost to the self brings sure healing.[50]

The soul which burns for sight of the supreme Love, who is God, suffers immensely in having to wait for that vision and at the same time this ardent expectation brings about a great purification. As Romano Guardini put it, for the soul in Purgatory, "his suffering is both the outcome of his condition and its cure".[51]

Something of this suffering-of-love may perhaps be gleaned from the experience of mystics in this life. In *Crossing the Threshold of Hope*, St John Paul II recounted:

> The mystical works of St John of the Cross offered me a very strong argument for purgatory. The 'living flame of love', of which St John of the Cross speaks, is above all a purifying fire. The mystical nights described by this great Doctor of the Church on the basis of his own experience correspond, in a certain sense, to purgatory. God makes man pass through such an interior purgatory of his sensual and spiritual nature in order to bring him into union with Himself.[52]

A Delay of Glory

The intense desire to behold God face-to-face which often figures in the poems of St John of the Cross may give some insight into the pain of the *dilatio gloriae* or "delay of glory" of Purgatory. For example in his *Songs between the soul and the bridegroom*, using nuptial imagery, St John of the Cross has the bride, the human soul, express its longing for Christ the bridegroom in these terms:

> Come, end my sufferings quite
> Since no one else suffices for physician:

And let my eyes have sight
Of you, who are their light,
Except for whom I scorn the gift of vision.

Reveal your presence clearly
And kill me with the beauty you discover,
For pains acquired so dearly
From Love, cannot recover
Save only through the presence of the lover.[53]

The notion of a physical suffering in Purgatory aside from the delay of glory, has always been present in Christian reflection on this mystery. The idea that there is also a "pain of sense" (*poenum sensi*) derives from the nature of sin. Given that all sins, including venial faults, involve not just a turning away from God (*aversio a Deo*), but also a disordered conversion towards creatures or created reality (*conversio ad creaturas*), it seems coherent that God would punish sinners not only "negatively", by withdrawing from them, but also "positively" through pain inflicted by a created reality. Usually this physical agent is identified as fire although extreme cold has also been suggested by some authors, including St Bernard (d.1153).[54]

The great Franciscan theologian, St Bonaventure (d. 1274) is echoing many Christian thinkers when he maintains that it is just that a spirit who subjects itself to a lesser good, through contempt of the supreme and eternal good, be in turn subjected to inferior goods and receive pains from those through whom he committed the crime and for whom he despised God and defiled himself.[55] Furthermore, the notion of a physical suffering is linked to the awareness that sin not only damages the sinner, but also creation itself.

This notion of a two-fold pain was also influenced at times by the comparison between Purgatory and hell. As the *Catechism of the Catholic Church* teaches, "the chief punishment of hell is eternal separation from God".[56] Along with this "pain of loss" (*poenum damni*), which is the eternal privation of God, from the Fathers onwards, it has been traditional to speak of an eternal *poenum sensi* or pain inflicted by some physical agent.

Not a Temporary Hell

The portrayal of Purgatory as a kind of temporary hell is very much to be avoided. The universal *Catechism* emphasises that "this final purification of the elect...is entirely different from the punishment of the damned". As St John Paul II put it when speaking about hope for eternal life: "Even if the soul in that passage towards heaven had to undergo purification for the remains of sin in purgatory, it is full of light, of certitude, of joy, because it is sure that it belongs to God forever".[57]

It is much more accurate to see Purgatory as the ante-chamber or waiting-room for heaven, where the souls are truly holy, are in love with God and embrace their final cleansing with profound gratitude as they prepare for communion with the Blessed Trinity. In the words of St Josemaria Escriva (d. 1975): "Purgatory shows God's great mercy and washes away the defects of those who long to become one with him."[58] In his *Purgatorio* (II, 75), part of his epic *La Divina Commedia*, Dante Alighieri describes Purgatory in the simple formula: *a farsi belli*, to bring humans under God's grace to the fullness of splendour and beauty.

Purgatorial Fire

The term *"ignis purgatorius"*, meaning a cleansing or purging fire, became consecrated in Catholic theology in the wake of St Augustine. Many other Fathers also speak of the fire of purification, especially in their commentaries on the text of 1 Corinthians 3:15. One could cite Sts Hilary, Cyprian, Gregory the Great, Gregory of Nyssa as well as Clement of Alexandria, among others. As the *Catechism of the Catholic Church* states: "the tradition of the Church, by reference to certain texts of Scripture, speaks of a cleansing fire".[59]

For centuries many theologians held that the purgatorial fire is real and physical, while in recent decades it is more common to interpret the fire in metaphorical terms. Certainly it is very difficult to understand how a material agent like fire could affect a spiritual reality such as the soul separated from the body. The most common solution offered to this quandary was that of St Thomas Aquinas who suggested that perhaps the fire purifies by means of a certain "restraining", "binding" or "limiting" of the separated soul. In other words, the soul would suffer by being somehow tied to a material agent such as fire.[60]

In his 2007 encyclical on Christian Hope, *Spe Salvi*, evoking the text of 1 Corinthians 3:12-15, Benedict XVI wrote:

> Some recent theologians are of the opinion that the fire which both burns and saves is Christ himself, the Judge and Saviour. The encounter with him is the decisive act of judgement. Before his gaze all falsehood melts away. This encounter with him, as it burns us, transforms and frees us, allowing us to become truly ourselves. All that we build during our lives can prove to be mere straw, pure bluster, and it collapses. Yet in the pain of this encounter, when the impurity and sickness of our lives become evident to us, there lies salvation. His gaze, the touch of his heart heals us through an undeniably painful transformation 'as through fire'. But it is a blessed pain, in which the holy power of his love sears through us like a flame, enabling us to become totally ourselves and thus totally of God. In this way the inter-relation between justice and grace also becomes clear: the way we live our lives is not

immaterial, but our defilement does not stain us for ever if we have at least continued to reach out towards Christ, towards truth and towards love.[61]

Purgatorial Fire and the Differences Between East and West

In the context of the fire of Purgatory something may be said of the complex history of differences with some Orthodox Christians regarding the teaching on purification after death. Some Eastern theologians opposed the idea of a purgatorial fire because they feared it was a return to the heresy of Origen known as the *apokatastasis* or universal reconciliation. Origen held that in the end all people would be saved by purification through fire, thereby denying Catholic teaching on the eternity of hell.

Some Eastern Christians also reacted against the conviction among Latin theologians regarding the existence of a real physical fire and the related notion of Purgatory being in a specific geographical location.

When in 1439 a successful but sadly short-lived attempt was made at the Council of Florence to re-establish doctrinal unity between Orthodox and Catholics, the theme of Purgatory was broached and a solemn definition given. For those who "are truly penitent and die in God's love before having satisfied by worthy fruits of penance for their sins", the conciliar decree states, "their souls are cleansed after death by purgatorial penalties (*poenis purgatoriis*); the acts of intercession (*suffragia*) of the living benefit them, namely the sacrifice of the Mass, prayers, alms, and other works of piety".[62]

Interestingly no mention is made either of the "fire" of Purgatory or of a geographical location.[63]

For Eastern authors Purgatory is not generally considered as a place where suffering is inflicted in expiation for sin. Instead, the living, through their prayer, almsgiving, and offering of the Eucharist, can obtain comfort for the souls in Purgatory. Rather than expiation of one's faults, purification tends to be seen as being alleviation from the affliction deserved by those faults.

All in all, and in spite of the various explanations given, the doctrine of *post-mortem* purification is pacifically accepted in the East.

"Location" and "Duration"

At times the nature of Purgatory and the state of the holy souls was conceived of in measurable and geographical terms. Some thought that Purgatory was located in a specific place underground, or between heaven and hell. It is interesting to note that the noun "Purgatory" (*purgatorium*) only emerged at the start of the second millennium, and was associated with the idea of a location. However, as St John Paul II taught, "the term 'purgatory' does not indicate a place but a condition of existence".[64]

What of the "duration" of Purgatory? This process of cleansing was sometimes regarded as measurable in terms of earthly time.

Many of the great scholastic theologians, including St Thomas Aquinas, referred instead to the concept of "aeviternity". Aeviternity is distinct both from "temporality" or chronological time in this world, and from "eternity", without beginning or end, which belongs only to God. Aeviternity is the measure proper to angels, and might also be applied to the souls in Purgatory. It has a beginning but not an end, since it is characteristic of beings who have been created at a particular moment in time, but are destined for everlasting life. It is a duration marked not by a series of physical changes and events, but by the succession of the soul's thoughts and affections.

The issue of the "duration" of Purgatory has come to the fore once again in recent decades because of the denial by some theologians of any intermediate phase between an individual's death and the end of the world.

These theories, sometimes referred to as "one-phase eschatologies", hold that at the moment of death each person enters immediately into the end of the world and the final universal judgement. This also implies that each person is resurrected bodily immediately after death. Hence there would be no period in which the soul is separated from the body. There would no distinction or gap between the particular judgement and the final judgement. In this view therefore, there would be no period or phase of Purgatory; any purgation required would take place at the one moment of death-judgement-resurrection.

The Maturation of Love

In its *Letter on certain questions concerning Eschatology* of May 1979, the Congregation for the Doctrine of the Faith recalled the urgent necessity of proclaiming the truth about everlasting life, and affirmed seven doctrinal points, some of which are especially relevant to Purgatory.[65]

The third affirmed the Church's belief "that a spiritual element survives and subsists after death, an element endowed with consciousness and will, so that the 'human self' subsists. To designate this element, the Church uses the word 'soul', the accepted term in the usage of Scripture and Tradition". The fourth "excludes every way of thinking or speaking that would render meaningless or unintelligible her prayers, her funeral rites, and the religious acts offered for the dead", while the fifth makes explicit that the end of time and the "glorious manifestation of our Lord" is "distinct and deferred with respect to the situation of people immediately after death".

Clearly, the question of the "duration" of Purgatory is mysterious and beyond what we can fully conceptualise. Nonetheless, this purification is related to time in some way, since it comes between two clear historical moments, namely the physical death of given individuals and the end of the world. If the second coming of Christ - his Parousia,[66] and the resurrection of the dead are yet to be awaited, a certain "time" after death must be taken into account even if this "duration" cannot be directly understood with earthly categories.

In any event the purification and sufferings of Purgatory are not uniform, since the Lord cares for each soul individually and "will render to every man according to his works" (*Rm* 2:6). St Thomas Aquinas speculated that the severity of the punishment corresponds to the gravity of the guilt, while its duration (*diuturnitas*) depends on how rooted sin is in the soul.[67] For his part Benedict XVI asserted that "the transforming 'moment' of encounter eludes earthly time-reckoning - it is the heart's time, it is the time of 'passage' to communion with God in the Body of Christ".[68]

Purgatory is the maturation of love. It is precisely because it is a mystery of love that Purgatory involves great suffering and great joy together. As St Catherine of Genoa puts it in her *Treatise*:

"There is no joy save that in paradise to be compared to the joy of the souls in purgatory...In contrast to this joy, this harmony with God's will also brings about a very great suffering. Its comprehension is beyond all words or thought...The overwhelming love of God gives it [the soul] joy beyond words. Yet this joy does not do away with one bit of pain in the suffering of the souls in purgatory. As the soul grows in its perfection, so does it suffer more because of what impedes the final consummation, the end for which God made it; so that in purgatory great joy and great suffering do not exclude one another."[69]

Purgatory and the Communion of the Saints

In the extensive 1980 interview published in English as *The Ratzinger Report*, the then-Cardinal Ratzinger stated: "My view is that if Purgatory did not exist, we should have to invent it". Why so? "Because few things are as immediate, as human and as widespread - at all times and in all cultures - as prayer for one's departed dear ones".[70]

This observation points to another essential aspect of Purgatory as a mystery of love. This dogma illumines how the three dimensions of the Church - heavenly, earthly and purgatorial - are all united in Christ and have an effective mutual communion. The fact that the living faithful can aid the dead, which is an essential part of the faith regarding Purgatory, sheds a particular light on the reality of the Church. This can be seen by a brief reference to some of the rich teachings on the Church from and since the Second Vatican Council.

Lumen Gentium teaches that God "willed to make men holy and save them, not as individuals without any bond or link between them, but rather to make them into a people".[71] Prayer for the dead is readily understood within the vision of the Church as the People of God.

The Church is a True Family

The union between the living and the dead is also a consequence of the fact that the Church is the Mystical Body of Christ, with a real organic unity between Head and members, and between the members themselves in and through Christ. As Pope Francis recalled:

> Church Tradition has always urged prayer for the deceased, in particular by offering the Eucharistic Celebration for them: it is the best spiritual help that we can give to their souls, particularly to those who are the most forsaken. The foundation of prayer in suffrage lies in the communion of the Mystical Body.[72]

The teaching on the living unity and mutual support of all members of the Body of Christ is found above all in the Letters of St Paul. "If one member suffers, all suffer together; if one member is honoured, all rejoice together. Now you are the body of Christ and individually members of it" (*1 Co* 12:26-27). Elsewhere the Apostle affirms that "none of us lives to himself, and none of us dies to himself" (*Rm* 14:7).[73]

Further, as St John Paul II pointed out at the end of his 1999 catechesis on Purgatory, the Church's teaching and praxis on Purgatory emphasises "the dimension of 'communio'", in other words, the Church understood as a communion, which is the principal understanding of the Church which has emerged since the Second Vatican Council.

This "communion of saints" which is the Church[74] is not limited to this life. Rather, said St John Paul II, "those, in fact, who find themselves in the state of purification are united both with the blessed who already enjoy the fullness of eternal life, and with us on earth on our way towards the Father's house".[75]

Purgatory is therefore a mystery of love also because the Church is a true family where "this solidarity with all men living or dead" means that "the least of our acts done in charity redounds to the profit of all".[76]

Suffrages: Ways in which the living can help the dead

Any act of charity can be an effective help to the holy souls, so there is an immense variety of suffrages. The principal aid, as is clear from the perennial practice and teaching of the Church, is the Eucharistic Sacrifice.[77] The celebration of the Eucharist offered for the dead testifies to the infinite value of the one perfect sacrifice of redemption (cf. *Heb* 10:11-18). It also shows the "propitiatory" dimension of the Mass, that is to say, the effectiveness of the Mass as a making-up for, or expiation of sin and a source of divine mercy.

In September of 1529, a few weeks before being appointed Lord Chancellor of England, St Thomas More wrote *The Supplication of Souls*. This vigorous defence of the existence of Purgatory, crafted with great humour and art, was a response to a pamphlet entitled *A Supplication for Beggars*, which had been published anonymously by Simon Fish in February of that year. In his tract, in which he appealed strongly to Henry VIII, Fish contended that all the problems of contemporary England had their origin in one source: the greed and corruption of the English clergy, including their insistence on being paid to pray for the dead.

More's defence of Purgatory is primarily scriptural and is greatly enhanced rhetorically by being put on the lips of the holy souls themselves. The persuasiveness of More's argument is suggested by the fact that Simon Fish, who perished a year later of the plague, died reconciled with the Church.

In countering the claim that there is no need to pray for the dead, the souls of Purgatory appeal directly to the reader:

> Think of our pains and take pity in your hearts, and help us with your prayers, pilgrimages and almsgivings. And most especially of all, procure for us the suffrages

and blessed oblation of the holy Mass, of which no one living can tell the fruit so well as we who here taste it.[78]

Indulgences

Other suffrages include a great variety of prayers and acts of penance or mortification, as well as almsgiving and pilgrimages. Many people have the custom of offering Rosaries or hours of work for the holy souls, while others live their times of hardship or illness in solidarity with them. As Benedict XVI pointed out, "the Church invites us to pray for them every day, also offering our daily sufferings and efforts so that, completely purified, they may be admitted to the eternal joy of light and peace in the Lord".[79]

The Church's teaching on indulgences has been expressed in recent times in the Apostolic Constitution *Indulgentiarum Doctrina* of 1st January 1967.[80] Here Blessed Paul VI shows that indulgences are "solidly founded on divine Revelation handed down by the apostles".[81] The "doctrine of Purgatory" is explicitly recalled since it "clearly demonstrates that even where the guilt of sin has been taken away, punishment for it or the consequences of it may remain to be expiated or cleansed".[82]

An indulgence "is a remission before God of the temporal punishment due to sins whose guilt has already been forgiven, which the faithful Christian who is duly disposed gains under certain prescribed conditions through the action of the Church which, as the minister of redemption, dispenses and applies with authority the treasure of the satisfactions of Christ and the saints".[83] "An indulgence is partial or plenary according as it removes either part or all of the temporal punishment due to sin".[84] A plenary indulgence may be gained only once a day.[85]

The heavenly, earthly and purgatorial Church are united in the praxis of indulgences. The infinite merits of Christ along with the prayers and good works of the Blessed Virgin Mary and all the saints form a common "treasury of the Church".[86] In virtue of this treasury and in a way regulated by the Church,[87] the faithful on earth can obtain indulgences for the souls of the departed. The intense "supernatural solidarity" between all the faithful of Christ, living and dead, means, says Blessed Paul VI, that there exists "an abundant exchange of all the goods by which divine justice is placated and expiation is made for the sins of the Mystical Body".[88]

Care for the Dead

One may obtain an indulgence for the dead or for oneself. The usual conditions include being in the state of grace, sacramental Confession and Holy Communion close to or on the day the indulgence is obtained, and being interiorly detached from sin. Indulgences are granted by the Church especially for Jubilee Years, such as the Great Jubilee of 2000 AD,[89] and on other special occasions such as the Year of Faith, the Year for Priests, the Pauline Year or the Year of Consecrated Life, or for particular gatherings or pilgrimages like World Youth Day or the World Meeting of Families. Other indulgences are available at all times when a particular prayer or good act is carried out, such as a period of Eucharistic adoration, the family Rosary, or the recitation of certain prayers.[90]

The care of the living for the dead is an aspect of the apostolic calling of all the baptised. Just as all the faithful are called to be "fishers of men" (*Mt* 4:19) by seeking to lead everyone to the Lord, helping the souls in Purgatory is another form of collaboration in the redemptive work of God who loves all souls (cf. *Ws* 11:26).

In St Thomas More's *Supplication of Souls*, those undergoing purification are at pains to stress the reality of Purgatory not only for their own sake, but also for the sake of the living. While appealing to the faithful on earth for their aid, the holy souls assure them that "there will also rebound upon yourselves an inestimable profit".[91]

To offer prayers and sacrifices for the deceased is a great work of charity and thus the one who offers suffrages grows in love, the greatest of all the virtues (*1 Co* 13:13). Charity for the dead reaches out to all including the most forgotten souls.

"We are called to remember everyone", teaches Pope Francis, "even those who no one remembers. We remember the victims of war and violence; the many 'little ones' of the world, crushed by hunger and poverty; we remember the anonymous who rest in common graves. We remember our brothers and sisters killed because they were Christian; and those who sacrificed their lives to serve others."[92]

When the time comes for the living faithful to pass through death they in turn will receive the grateful support of those for whom they had mercy in their time of need. St Thomas More's holy souls use a metaphor to explain this:

> For just as when you light a candle for someone else, you have no less light for yourself, and when you blow on a fire to warm someone else, you also warm yourself with it, so, good friends, surely the good that you send here before you both greatly refreshes us and still is wholly preserved here for you, with our prayers added to it for your further advantage.[93]

The Help of the Heavenly Church

In the family of the Church, those who are already safely home are in the best position to help those still on their journey. The saints and angels pray not only for the living faithful but also for those undergoing the final purification before entry to heaven. The holy souls are greatly helped by the intercession of those already in heaven.

The Liturgy testifies to the awareness of the Church in this regard, such as in the following Collect prayer from a Mass for the dead in the Roman Missal:

O God, giver of pardon and loving author of
    our salvation,
grant, we pray you, in your mercy,
that, through the intercession
of Blessed Mary, ever-Virgin, and all your Saints,
the members, friends, and benefactors of
    our community,
who have passed from this world,
may attain a share in eternal happiness.[94]

The Blessed Virgin is foremost in praying for the holy souls, continuing the maternal care she lavished on them during their earthly lives. In St Thomas More's tract, the souls in Purgatory tell of the support of the heavenly Church in these terms:

The comfort that we have here, other than our continual hope in our Lord God, comes at times from our Lady, along with such glorious saints as either we ourselves, through our own devotion when we were alive, or you, with yours on our behalf after our death and departure, have made intercessors for us.[95]

Angels

The souls of the *Supplication* also speak of the consolation received from the angels:

> And among others, most especially we are beholden to those blessed spirits, our very own good angels. When we behold them coming with comfort to us, we take great pleasure and greatly rejoice in this.[96]

The special role of angels at the moment of a Christian's death and in accompanying the soul towards God has a biblical basis[97] and is strongly asserted in the writings of the Fathers of the Church.[98] Sts Bernardine of Siena, Catherine of Genoa, Francis de Sales and Blessed John Henry Newman, have all taken up this tradition. For his part Dante Alighieri depicts angels bringing souls on ships to Purgatory in Canto II of his *Purgatorio*.

The Dream of Gerontius

Perhaps the most beautiful literary expression of the relationship between the angels and Purgatory is found in Blessed John Henry Newman's *The Dream of Gerontius*. Newman wrote this longest and most successful of his poems in 1865, and it captivated Catholics and non-Catholics alike from the start. The composer Edward Elgar put *The Dream* to music in 1900 and it became his best choral and orchestral work.[99]

This poem traces the progress of the soul of the elderly man *Gerontius* from the moment of his death to his particular judgement and his subsequent entry to Purgatory. The text is made the more dramatic by the fact that it is largely composed of the dialogue between the soul of Gerontius and his guardian angel.

In this progress of the soul from the body towards judgement we hear the prayers and litanies of those gathered about Gerontius's death-bed and the final commendation prayed by the priest, as well as the hymns and prayers of various angels and angelic choirs, and of the souls of Purgatory. The poem is marked by the great tenderness of the guardian angel for the soul entrusted to its care, which contrasts with the brief and insulting words of the demons.

After his particular judgement, the old man's soul is handed over to the Angels of Purgatory for its final purification. The great poem ends serenely with the temporary farewell to Gerontius by his guardian angel:

Softly and gently, dearest, sweetest soul,
In my most loving arms I now enfold thee,
And, o'er the penal waters, as they roll,
I poise thee, and I lower thee, and hold thee.
And carefully I dip thee in the lake,

And thou, without a sob or a resistance,
Dost through the flood thy rapid passage take,

Sinking deep, deeper, into the dim distance.
Angels, to whom the willing task is given,

Shall tend, and nurse, and lull thee as thou liest;
And Masses on the earth, and prayers in heaven,
Shall aid thee at the Throne of the Most Highest.
Farewell, but not forever! Brother dear,

Be brave and patient on thy bed of sorrow;
Swiftly shall pass thy night of trial here,
And I will come and wake thee on the morrow.

The Prayer of the Holy Souls

It seems clear that the holy souls can and do pray. Their
loving existence and sufferings constitute a prayer.
The question has often been asked whether they can
intercede for the living. St Thomas Aquinas wrote that
the souls underdoing this final purification are in a state
"more to be prayed for" than to be praying,[100] and some
authors took this as a straight negative response to the
question. However while it is clear that the holy souls
have a deep need for the prayer of the heavenly and
earthly Church, this does not necessarily mean that they
cannot pray for the living.

It would seem to make sense that they do pray for the
living. They are joined by love with the entire Mystical
Body of Christ. After stating that "all, indeed, who are of
Christ and who have his Spirit form one Church and in

Christ cleave together (cf. *Ep* 4:16)", the Second Vatican Council goes on to affirm: "So it is that the union of the wayfarers with the brethren who sleep in Christ is in no way interrupted, but on the contrary, according to the constant faith of the Church, this union is reinforced by an exchange of spiritual goods".[101]

The Church has not definitively taught on this question, nor has she rebuked the common practice among the faithful of praying to the souls in Purgatory. A proposal to include an explicit reference to entrusting oneself to the prayers of the holy souls and their intercession for the living, was removed from an earlier draft of *Lumen Gentium* as the council did not wish to declare on this point.

For its part, the *Catechism of the Catholic Church* 958 states that "our prayer for them [the holy souls] is capable not only of helping them, but also of making their intercession for us effective".[102] Thus the *Catechism* places our prayer for the dead to the fore, while affirming also their intercession.

The Holy Souls, Our "Good Friends"

The devotion of St Josemaria Escriva to the holy souls reflects a common attitude of the faithful in this regard over many centuries. The founder of Opus Dei liked to refer to the souls in Purgatory as his "good friends", thereby implying reciprocal love and support. Indeed while he was always very generous in offering suffrages for the dead, especially in the celebration of Mass, he entrusted particular intentions to them and asked them for favours for his daily work and apostolate.

Hailed by St John Paul II as "the saint of ordinary life",[103] St Josemaria sought to encourage ordinary Christians to be contemplatives in the middle of the world and in this context to develop an ongoing relationship with the entire communion of saints, including the angels and saints, and the souls in Purgatory. In his spiritual classic *The Way* (n. 571) he writes very characteristically:

> The holy Souls in purgatory. Out of charity, out of justice, and out of excusable selfishness - they have such power with God! - remember them often in your sacrifices and in your prayers. May you be able to say when you speak of them, 'My good friends the souls in purgatory'.

Conclusion

This brief consideration of the mystery of Purgatory brings to light many aspects of the Catholic Faith, including the realities of sin and redemption, merit, satisfaction, freedom and grace, the universal call to holiness and God's desire for "all men to be saved and to come to the knowledge of the truth" (*1 Tm* 2:4).

The reality of purification in the next life also highlights the great dignity of being called to communion with God through Christ, and the importance of having a healthy "sense of sin" so as to be able to understand God's mercy.[104] The eternal Father offers a final cleansing to his beloved children so that they may reach "mature manhood, to the measure of the fullness of the stature of Christ" (*Ep* 4:13).

Above all else, Purgatory is about the triumph of love. The human being comes to embrace God's love freely and fully, and God who always loves us first (cf. *1 Jn* 4:10-19), through his great mercy prepares us for the everlasting embrace of divine love. To reflect on Purgatory is to face towards heaven.

The dogma of Purgatory also shows how the Church is a loving family with real mutual support between all members. Care for the dead on the part of the living is an important act of charity.

We finish with some words of Pope Francis from All Souls' Day in 2014:

With this faith in man's supreme destiny, we now turn to Our Lady, who suffered the tragedy of Christ's death beneath the Cross and took part in the joy of his Resurrection. May she, the *Gate of Heaven*, help us to understand more and more the value of prayer in suffrage for the souls of the dead. They are close to us! May she support us on our daily pilgrimage on earth and help us to never lose sight of life's ultimate goal which is Heaven.[105]

Further Reading

Church Teaching

Second Vatican Council, Dogmatic Constitution on the Church, *Lumen Gentium*, 21st November 1964, chapter 7, especially 48-50 (*Acta Apostolicae Sedis* [AAS] 57 (1965), 5-75).

Paul VI, Apostolic Constitution on the Revision of Indulgences, *Indulgentiarum Doctrina*, 1st January 1967 ([AAS] 59 (1967), 5-24); The Creed of the People of God, *Sollemnis Professio Fidei*, 30th June 1968, 28 ([AAS] 60 (1968), 433-446).

St John Paul II, Catechesis at General Audience, 4th August 1999; Message for the Millennium of All Souls Day, 2nd June 1998.

Benedict XVI, Encyclical on Christian Hope, *Spe Salvi*, 30th November 2007, 45-48 ([AAS] 99 (2007), 985-1027).

Francis, Angelus, 2nd November 2014; Homilies at the *Verano* Cemetery, Rome, 1st November 2013, and 1st November 2014.

Sacred Congregation for the Doctrine of the Faith, Letter on certain questions concerning Eschatology, *Recentiores*, 17th May 1979.

Catechism of the Catholic Church 1030-1032, 1054 (Purgatory); 1471-1479, 1498 (Indulgences).

Saints

St Catherine of Genoa, *Purgation and Purgatory* (New Jersey: Paulist Press, 1979).

St Josemaria Escriva, *The Way* 571, 898, 899; *Furrow* 889; *The Forge* 1041, 1046 (New York: Scepter, 2002).

St Thomas More, *The Supplication of Souls* (New York, Scepter, 2002).

Blessed John Henry Newman, Sermon on "Holiness necessary for future Blessedness", in *Parochial and Plain Sermons* (London, Green and Co., 1891), vol. 1, pp. 1-14; *The Dream of Gerontius* (Oxford, Family Publications, 2001).

Theology

R. Garrigou-Lagrange OP, *Life Everlasting and the Immensity of the Soul* (Rockford, Illinois, Tan Books, 1952), pp. 147-201.

R. Guardini, *Eternal Life* (New Hampshire, Sophia Institute Press, 1998), pp. 33-54.

P. O'Callaghan, *Christ our Hope. An Introduction to Eschatology* (Washington D.C., The Catholic University of America Press, 2011), pp. 286-308.

J.T. O'Connor, *Land of the Living. A Theology of the Last Things* (New York, Catholic Book Publishing Co., 1992), pp. 30, 127, 131.

C. Pozo, SJ, *Theology of the Beyond* (New York, St Paul's, 2009), pp. 455-476.

J. Ratzinger, *Eschatology. Death and Eternal Life* (Washington D.C., The Catholic University of America Press, 2007), pp. 218-233.

Endnotes

[1] Cf. *Catechism of the Catholic Church* 460. Church documents cited throughout this text, including papal teaching (encyclicals, apostolic exhortations, homilies and audiences), the documents of the Second Vatican Council, and the *Catechism of the Catholic Church* are all available on the website of the Holy See: *http://w2.vatican.va/content/vatican/en.html*.

[2] Second Vatican Council, *Lumen Gentium* 40.

[3] St John Paul II, Catechesis on Purgatory, Audience, 4th August 1999.

[4] Benedict XVI, Homily, Mass with his former university students, Castel Gandolfo, 30th August 2009.

[5] Benedict XVI, Angelus, 1st November 2005.

[6] St John Paul II, Catechesis on Purgatory, Audience, 4th August 1999.

[7] Cf. Lev 11:44; Dt 7:6; Is 1:4, 5:19.

[8] Cf. Lev 19:2, 20:26; Mt 5:48.

[9] Cf. also Ps 24:3-6; Is 33:13-16.

[10] Cf. St John Paul II, Catechesis on Purgatory, Audience, 4th August 1999, 2, where the Holy Father referred to the "Old Testament religious law [where] what is destined for God must be perfect".

58

[11] Cf. Ep 1:4; 1 Th 2:3.

[12] Blessed John Henry Newman, "Sermon on the Holiness necessary for future Blessedness", *Parochial and Plain Sermons*, (London, Green and Co., 1891), Volume 1, pp. 1-14.

[13] Cf. 1 Jn 3:1-3.

[14] *Catechism of the Catholic Church* 1054.

[15] Cf. 2 S 12:7.

[16] Cf. Jn 21:15-17.

[17] Cf. Jn 18:17. 25-27.

[18] *Catechism of the Catholic Church* 1472. Cf. also 1459.

[19] *Catechism of the Catholic Church* 1472.

[20] For example, in his will, St Ephrem asks not for funeral pomp but for prayers and sacrifices after the example of Judas Maccabeus, while St Augustine mentions 2 Maccabees 12 in relation to the custom of the universal Church in praying for the dead.

[21] Cf. Vatican II, *Lumen Gentium*, 50; Benedict XVI, Encyclical, *Spe Salvi*, 30th November 2007, 48; *Catechism of the Catholic Church* 1032.

[22] Cf. Benedict XVI's meditation on 1 Corinthians 3:12-15 in his Encyclical, *Spe Salvi*, 30th November 2007, 46-47.

[23] Cf. St Augustine, *City of God*, XXI, 24, 2, and St Gregory the Great, *Dialogues*, IV, 39.

[24] Cf. St Robert Bellarmine, *De Purgatorio*, I, 8.

[25] The adjective "patristic" refers to the reflection of the Fathers of the Church, and derives from the Latin word *"pater"* meaning "father".

[26] Tertullian, St Augustine and St Gregory the Great may be cited in this context.

[27] *Passio Ss Perpetuae et Felicitatis* (sometimes attributed to Tertullian).

[28] Tertullian, *De Monogamia*, 10.

[29] St Jerome, *Epistula 66, ad Pammachium*.

[30] J. Ratzinger, *Eschatology:. Death and Eternal Life* (Washington D.C., Catholic University of American Press, 2007), p. 226. This eschatology textbook is the fruit of J. Ratzinger's years of lecturing on the subject.

[31] *Catechism of the Catholic Church* 1124.

[32] St Cyril of Jerusalem, *Catechesis Mystagogica*, V, 9.

[33] St Augustine, *Confessions* IX, 27, 32.

[34] Cf. Council of Florence, Bull *Laetentur caeli*, 6th July 1439; Council of Trent, Decree *De Purgatorio*, 3rd-4th December 1563.

[35] Cf. H. Leclerq, "Purgatoire", in *Dictionnaire d'archéologie chrétienne et de liturgie* (Paris, Letouzey, 1948), Volume XIV/2, column 1979.

[36] Roman Missal, Eucharistic Prayer I (The Roman Canon).

[37] Council of Trent, Decree *de Iustificatione*, 13th January 1547, Canon 30. In his Apostolic Exhortation on Reconciliation and Penance in the Mission of the Church today, *Reconciliatio et Poenitentia*, 2nd December 1984, 17, St John Paul II recalls that temporal punishment "can be expiated on earth or in purgatory".

[38] Council of Trent, Decree *de Purgatorio*, 3rd-4th December 1563. Trent also refers to Purgatory in Session XXII (17th September 1562) when it speaks of the Sacrifice of the Mass offered for the dead. The Second Vatican Council references Trent's Decree *de Purgatorio* in *Lumen Gentium* 51.

[39] Council of Trent, Decree *de Purgatorio*, 3rd-4th December 1563.

[40] Second Vatican Council, *Gaudium et Spes* 18.

[41] St John Paul II, Apostolic Letter at the Close of the Great Jubilee of the Year 2000, *Novo Millenio Ineunte*, 6th January 2001, 27.

[42] *Catechism of the Catholic Church* 1022.

[43] *Catechism of the Catholic Church* 1022.

[44] Cf. *Catechism of the Catholic Church* 2006-2011.

[45] *Catechism of the Catholic Church* 1021.

[46] Cf. St Robert Bellarmine, *De Purgatorio*, II, 3.

[47] For a recent edition, cf. St Catherine of Genoa, *Purgation and Purgatory* (New Jersey, Paulist Press, 1979).

[48] Benedict XVI, Audience, 12th January 2011.

[49] St Catherine of Genoa, *Purgation and Purgatory*, p. 81.

[50] F. Sheed, *Theology for Beginners* (London, Sheed and Ward [Stagbooks], 2001), p. 175.

[51] R. Guardini, *Eternal Life* (New Hampshire, Sophia Press, 1998), p. 52.

[52] St John Paul II, *Crossing the Threshold of Hope* (London, Random House, 1994), pp. 186-187.

[53] St John of the Cross, *Poems* [The Spanish text with a translation by R. Campbell], (Glasgow, William Collins Sons, 1981), p. 17: *Canciones entre el alma y el Esposo.*

[54] Cf. St Bernard, *Sermo 42 de quinque regionibus.*

[55] Cf. St Bonaventure, *Breviloquium*, VII, 2.

[56] *Catechism of the Catholic Church* 1035.

[57] St John Paul II, Audience: "The Holy Spirit, guarantee of eschatological hope and of final perseverance", 3rd July 1991.

[58] St Josemaria Escriva, *Furrow* 889.

[59] *Catechism of the Catholic Church* 1031.

[60] Cf. St Thomas Aquinas, *Supplementum*, q. 70, a. 3 c.

[61] Benedict XVI, Encyclical on Christian Hope, *Spe Salvi*, 30th November 2007, 47.

[62] Council of Florence, Decree for the Greeks (*Decretum pro Graecis*).

[63] On two earlier occasions the Church spoke of Purgatory and made no mention of purgatorial "fire": the Second Council of Lyons (1274), which like Florence achieved a restoration of doctrinal unity between East and West, although short-lived; and Benedict XII's constitution *Benedictus Deus* (1336). Some minor Church documents of the Middle Ages, however do mention the "fire" of Purgatory, specifically the Letters *Sub catholica professione* (1254) of Pope Innocent IV, and *Super quibusdam* (1351) of Pope Clement VI. More recently in n. 28 of the *Creed of the People of God* solemnly professed by Blessed Paul VI on 30th June 1968 at the conclusion of the Year of Faith, the Holy Father made reference to the "fire" of Purgatory in the Latin text. The English translation does not mention a fire, but simply refers to souls "purified in purgatory". The Latin reads: *"Credimus vitam aeternam. Credimus animas eorum omnium, qui in gratia moriuntur – sive quae adhuc Purgatorii igne expiandae sunt, sive quae statim ac corpore separatae, sicut Bonus Latro, a Iesu suscipiuntur – Populum Dei constituere post mortem".* (I underline)

[64] St John Paul II, Audience, 4th August 1999.

[65] Sacred Congregation for the Doctrine of the Faith, Letter on certain questions concerning Eschatology, *Recentiores*, 17th May 1979.

[66] Cf. *Catechism of the Catholic Church* 673-674, 681-682.

[67] Cf. St Thomas Aquinas, *In IV Sent.*, d. 21, q.1, a.3, qª. 3, ad 1.

[68] Benedict XVI, Encyclical on Christian Hope, *Spe Salvi*, 30th November 2007, 47.

[69] St Catherine of Genoa, *Purgation and Purgatory*, pp. 72, 81-82.

[70] J. Ratzinger with Vittorio Messori, *The Ratzinger Report: An exclusive interview on the state of the Church* (San Francisco, Ignatius Press, 1985), p. 146.

[71] Second Vatican Council, *Lumen Gentium* 9.

[72] Francis, Angelus, 2nd November 2014.

[73] Cf. *Catechism of the Catholic Church* 953, 1474

[74] Cf. *Catechism of the Catholic Church* 946, 960.

[75] St John Paul II, Audience, 4th August 1999, 6.

[76] *Catechism of the Catholic Church* 953.

[77] Cf. *Catechism of the Catholic Church* 1371.

[78] St Thomas More, *The Supplication of Souls* (New Jersey, Scepter, 2002), p. 192.

[79] Benedict XVI, Angelus, 1st November 2007.

[80] The doctrine of Paul VI's *Indulgentiarum Doctrina* is taken up in the *Catechism of the Catholic Church* 1471-1479, within its treatment of the Sacrament of Penance and Reconciliation. Cf. *Code of Canon Law*, canons 992-997.

[81] Paul VI, Apostolic Constitution *Indulgentiarum Doctrina*, 1st January 1967, 1.

[82] Paul VI, Apostolic Constitution *Indulgentiarum Doctrina*, 1st January 1967, 3.

[83] Paul VI, Apostolic Constitution *Indulgentiarum Doctrina*, 1st January 1967, Norm 1.

[84] Paul VI, Apostolic Constitution *Indulgentiarum Doctrina*, 1st January 1967, Norm 2. Cf. Norm 3.

[85] Cf. Apostolic Penitentiary, *The Gift of the Indulgence*, 29th January 2000, 4.

[86] Paul VI, Apostolic Constitution *Indulgentiarum Doctrina*, 1st January 1967, 4.

[87] Cf. *Catechism of the Catholic Church* 1478-1479.

[88] Paul VI, Apostolic Constitution *Indulgentiarum Doctrina*, 1st January 1967, 4.

[89] Cf. Apostolic Penitentiary, *The Gift of the Indulgence*, 29th January 2000.

[90] The list of indulgenced prayers and acts is contained in the Apostolic Penitentiary's *Enchiridion Indulgentiarum*, 4th Edition, Rome, 16th July 1999. For an English translation, cf. *Manual of Indulgences: norms and grants* (Washington D.C., USCCCB Publishing, 2006).

[91] St Thomas More, *The Supplication of Souls* (New Jersey, Scepter, 2002), p. 193.

[92] Francis, Angelus, 2nd November 2014.

[93] St Thomas More, *The Supplication of Souls* (New Jersey, Scepter, 2002), p. 184.

[94] *Roman Missal*, Various Prayers for the Dead, 12: For Relatives, Friends, and Benefactors.

[95] St Thomas More, *The Supplication of Souls* (New Jersey, Scepter, 2002), p. 192.

[96] St Thomas More, *The Supplication of Souls* (New Jersey, Scepter, 2002), p. 192.

[97] Luke 16:22: "The poor man [Lazarus] died and was carried by the angels to Abraham's bosom."

[98] Cf. J. Daniélou, SJ, *The Angels and their Mission, according to the Fathers of the Church* (Indiana, Ave Maria Press, 1957), Chapter 9: "The Angels and Death", pp. 95-105.

[99] Cf. J.H. Newman, *The Dream of Gerontius* (Oxford, Family Publications, 2001). This edition, which includes short introductions to Newman's poem and Elgar's composition, was published to mark the bicentenary of Newman's birth in 1801 and the centenary of the first performance of Elgar's masterpiece in 1900.

[100] St Thomas Aquinas, *Summa Theologiae* II-II, q. 83, a. 11, ad 3: *"Illi qui sunt in purgatorio, esti sint superiors nobis propter impeccabilitatem, sunt tamen inferiores quantum ad poenas, quas patitur, et secundum hoc non sunt in statu orandi, sed magis ut oretur pro eis".* (I underline)

[101] Second Vatican Council, *Lumen Gentium* 49.

[102] *The Catechism of Christian Doctrine of St Pius X* (n. 123): "The blessed in heaven and the souls in purgatory form a part of the communion of saints, because they are joined to each other and with us by charity, because those in paradise receive our prayers, and those in purgatory our assistance, and because they all repay us with their intercession with God on our behalf".

[103] St John Paul II, Audience, 7th October 2002.

[104] St John Paul II spoke of the "loss of the sense of sin" in his Apostolic Exhortation *Reconciliatio et Poenitentia* on Reconciliation and Penance in the mission of the Church today, 2nd December 1984, 18.

[105] Francis, Angelus, 2nd November 2014.

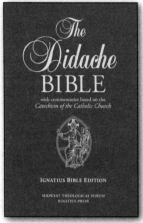

LIGHTHOUSE TALKS™

CAN YOU TRUST GOD?
DR. TIM GRAY

Dr. Gray addresses the pervasive misconceptions that God is quick to anger, that the God of the Old and New Testaments are different, and that God doesn't have a merciful heart for us.

MEN AND WOMEN ARE FROM EDEN
DR. MARY HEALY

With incredible clarity, Dr. Healy explains how the *Theology of the Body* is astonishingly good news for a culture littered with broken marriages, immorality, heartache, and loneliness.

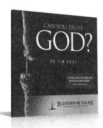

DISCOVER WHY LIGHTHOUSE TALKS HAVE REACHED
MORE THAN 15 MILLION LISTENERS ACROSS THE GLOBE

To learn more, visit us at
augustineinstitute.org/audio
or call (866) 767-3155

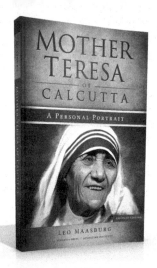

MOTHER TERESA OF CALCUTTA

FR. LEO MAASBURG

In this personal portrait of the beloved St. Teresa of Calcutta, Fr. Maasburg presents amazing stories about her that he was privileged to experience at her side. They all tell of her limitless trust in God's love, of the way the power of faith can move mountains, and of hope that can never die.

BROWSE SOME OF OUR MOST POPULAR BOOKS
AND SEE OUR COMPREHENSIVE LIST OF TITLES

Visit us at augustineinstitute.org/books
or call (866) 767-3155

CATHOLIC STUDY BIBLE APP

SCRIPTURE IN THE PALM OF YOUR HAND

The entire Catholic Bible (RSV-2CE) can be downloaded
for free! Packed with additional content from the Augustine
Institute, Ignatius Press, and other Catholic apostolates, this
app unlocks the beauty and richness of Scripture.

 iPad iPhone iPod touch  Google play kindle fire

This incredible **free** app brings the Bible to life!

- Complete text of the Old and New Testaments (RSV-2CE)
- Truth & Life™ Dramatized Audio New Testament—
  free Gospel of John
- 10 hours of **free** audio commentary from Dr. Scott Hahn
- Over 140 Lighthouse Talks

**Download now by searching for Catholic Study Bible
in the App Store**